GEN Z HUMOR

IRENE XANDERENA

GEN Z HUMOR
Copyright © 2023, Irene Xanderena
All Rights Reserved.

ISBN: 979-8-8690-8515-3

Published by
Eyereneeswords
Email: life@eyereneeswords.com
Website: www.eyereneeswords.com

CONTENT

ACKNOWLEDGMENT

Before diving into the hilarity of this Gen Z humor book, I feel the need to express my gratitude to a few key individuals who have made this wild journey possible. My Amazing children, Zander and Dreamer, my nieces, my nephews, my godsons, my goddaughters, and Gen Zers around the globe.

To my family and friends, thank you for being my sounding board for all the ridiculous jokes I've come up with. Your laughter (or groans) have been a constant source of validation. I appreciate your willingness to test out my jokes on unsuspecting victims and for pretending to find them funny even when they were just mildly amusing. You're the real MVPs.

A special shoutout goes to the internet, without which this book would not exist. You've been my ultimate muse. You've shown me that humor knows no bounds and that even the most obscure references can generate belly laughs. Thank you for being the weird and wonderful place where I find my daily dose of absurdity. I must also acknowledge the countless hours I've spent procrastinating on social media platforms in the name of "research." To Instagram, Snapchat, X, Threads, and TikTok, I owe you my sincerest gratitude especially for the times I neglected real-life responsibilities to cultivate my joke collection.

Last but certainly not least, I want to express my gratitude to all the readers who have picked up this book. Whether you're a Gen Zer, a younger or older generation trying to decode Gen Z's strange sense of humor or just someone who enjoys a good laugh, I appreciate you giving this humor book a chance. I hope this book brings a smile to your face and a chuckle to your soul. So, thank you, from the bottom of my heart, for joining me on this hilarious journey through the world of Gen Z humor. Let's laugh, connect, and embrace the weirdness together. It's going to be one heck of a ride!

INTRODUCTION

Hey there, fellow humans! So, here's the deal: I'm writing a Gen Z humor book. Why, you ask? Well, besides the fact that I have lived with them, there are a few reasons why I've decided to embark on this comedic adventure. Firstly, as the first generation to grow up fully immersed in the digital age, I've come to accept that their brain operates on a completely different frequency than other generations.

Gen Z refers to individuals who were born between the mid-1990s and early 2010s. They are the generation that follows the Millennials (also known as Gen Y). Gen Z individuals are often characterized by their familiarity with technology, their diverse and inclusive mindset, and their ability to adapt to a rapidly changing world. They have grown up in an era of social media, smartphones, and constant connectivity, which has influenced their attitudes, behaviors, and perspectives.

I mean, one moment they are laughing hysterically at a video of a cat playing the piano, and the next pondering the meaning of the universe while eating a bag of chips in pajamas. Secondly, I've noticed that people from older generations often give Gen Zers puzzled looks when they crack a joke or share a meme. It's like trying to decode an alien language! So, I thought, why not bridge the generation gap through laughter? Let's bring everyone together with a book that showcases the humor that unites us all, regardless of our age.

And hey, let's not forget the fact that Gen Z humor is downright hilarious. So, in this book, get ready to dive into the depths of Gen Z comedy. We'll explore the quirks of the generation, from their obsession with avocado toast to their love-hate relationship with technology. Whether you're a Gen Zer yourself, a curious parent trying to decode your kid's humor, or just looking for a good laugh, this book is for you. So, buckle up, get your emoji game on point, and let's embark on an adventure through the wonderfully weird world of Gen Z humor.

PREFACE

Greetings, fellow humans, aliens, and sentient beings from other dimensions! Welcome to this ridiculously entertaining book that explores the mind-boggling world of Gen Z humor. So, why did I decide to embark on this wild endeavor? Gather 'round, and I shall reveal the unabridged, utterly nonsensical tale behind it all.

Picture this: It was a regular day in my life, filled with existential crises, I aimlessly scrolled through my social media feeds, and I stumbled upon a meme so hilariously relatable that I snorted milk out of my nose. Yes, it was that good. At that moment, I thought, "Why not capture the essence of Gen Z humor in a book?!" So, I set forth on this epic quest to curate the most absurd, bizarre, and side-splittingly funny collection of Gen Z humor. I delved into the depths of the internet, desperately trying to understand what goes on in a Gen Z's brain.

As I ventured deeper into this comedic rabbit hole, I discovered a world teeming with tikis, yeets, and an entire dictionary's worth of slang that I still can't fully comprehend. But fear not, dear reader! I've taken it upon myself to translate this mysterious language of LOLs, ROFLs, and LMAOs into something that even your great-grandma can giggle at.

Now, before you embark on this journey with me, I must issue a warning: This book contains copious amounts of sarcasm, pop culture references, and enough memes to break the internet (again).

So, if you're allergic to laughter, have a phobia of puns, or simply can't handle the sheer brilliance of Gen Z humor, I suggest you put this book down immediately and seek professional help. But for those brave souls who are ready to dive headfirst into the world of Gen Z humor, buckle up! Get ready to snort, cackle, and possibly question your life choices as we embark on this outrageous adventure together. It's time to unleash the power of Gen Z humor upon the world!

DISCLAIMER

The author accepts no responsibility for any injuries, tears of laughter, or sudden urge to communicate solely through emojis that may occur while reading this book. Approach with caution, a good sense of humor, and a spare pair of underpants, just in case.

xviii

GEN Z HUMOR

1

How did the Gen Z person respond when asked if they are part of the Gen Z generation?

I don't identify as any generation!

2

What did the Gen Z person complain about?

I asked my phone for directions, and it replied: "Keep going straight until you reach your destination."

3

How does the Gez Z person voice their frustrations?

I tried to take a selfie, but my front camera said: "Sorry, I can't find your face."

4

What does the Gen Z person think about commitment?

"I asked my smartwatch if it loved me, and it replied: 'I only have time for you.' Well, that's one way to avoid commitment!

5

What is the Gen Zers' disposition?

I can't decide if I'm a night owl or an early bird. So, I guess that makes me some form of permanently exhausted pigeon.

6

What does the Gen Z person say about dating?

I was complaining about being single, and my friend said: "Don't worry, you're like a limited edition — everyone wants you, but no one can afford you." I guess I'm a collector's item now!

7

What does the Gen Z person think about procrastination?

If procrastination was a sport, I'd probably compete in it next week.

8

How does the Gen Z person
feel about being seen in
public with parents?

"I asked my parents if I could
go out, and they said: "Only
if you take us with you.'
Thanks, but I'll stay home!"

9

What is the Gen Z's take on stoicism?

When life gives you lemons, no problem, just date someone whose life gave them vodka!

10

How does the Gen Z plan out their life goals?

I finally got my life together, and now I can't remember where I put it.

11

Where does the Gen Z person get their motivation?

I told my computer I needed a motivational quote, and it replied: "Error 404: Motivation not found"

12

How does an angry Gen Z person count to 10?

1, 2, 3, 4, 5, 6, 7, 8, 9, "Ugh, whatever!"

13

Why did the Gen Z person become a chef?

So they could have a legitimate reason to say, "I'm cooking with rage!"

14

How does a Gen Z person apologize?

They send a text saying, "Sorry, not sorry.

15

How does an irritated Gen Z person communicate?

Through a series of eye rolls, sighs, and ughs.

16

How does a Gen Z person make a grocery list?

They create a TikTok dance routine with all the items they need!

17

Why did the Gen Z person become a stand-up comedian?

Because they thought laughter was the best way to "trend"!

18

How does a hilarious Gen Z
person order a pizza?

They ask the delivery person
to "slide into their DMs" with
a pepperoni surprise!

19

Why did the Gen Z person become a detective?

Because they always wanted to get to the "unbiased" truth!

20

How does the Gen Z person handle a broken phone?

They will just invent another device!

21

Why did the Gen Z person become a weather forecaster?

Because they refuse to assume it's sunny until they see the actual sun!

22

How does the Gen Z person order food at a restaurant?

They ask the waiter to describe every dish in detail. They have to google the taste first!

23

How does the Gen Z person react to a surprise party?

They won't assume it's for them until they see their name on the birthday cake! Then they say "Oh cool, I guess!"

24

How does the Gen Z person react to a text message?

They won't assume the sender's tone until they've analyzed every single emoji!

25

Why did the Gen Z person
join a debate club?

Because they thought it
would be a great opportunity
to practice not caring about
winning or losing!

26

How does the Gen Z person react to a compliment?

They'll just mumble, "Thanks, I guess," without any enthusiasm.

27

Why did the Gen Z person become a pet owner?

Because they wanted a furry friend who wouldn't mind if they forgot to feed them or take them for walks!

28

How does the Gen Z person react to bad news?

They'll just say, "Oh well, life goes on," without showing any other response.

29

Why did the Gen Z
person become a weather
forecaster?

So they could say, "Looks
like it might rain, but what
do I know? I'm just reading
a screen."

30

How does the Gen Z person handle criticism?

They'll respond with a smile and say, "Wow, thanks for your input. I'll definitely consider it...NOT!"

31

Why did the Gen Z person become a teacher?

So they could say, "I'm here to teach you, but who am I to tell you what's right or wrong?"

32

How does the Gen
Z person handle an
annoying neighbor?

They'll leave a note saying,
"Thanks for the constant
noise. I'm thrilled to be your
unintentional roommate!

33

How to recognize a Gen Z person:

They're constantly attached to their phone but somehow manage to have a full social life offline too.

34

You know you are speaking with a Gen Zer when:

Their vocabulary is a mix of real words, acronyms, and made-up slang. It's like trying to decipher a secret language only they understand.

35

How do you know your employee is a Gen Zer?

They can't understand why anyone would still use email when there are countless messaging apps available.

36

How can you spot a Gen Z human?

They can navigate through a video game with lightning speed and precision, but struggle to assemble basic furniture from IKEA.

37

How can you identify a Gen Z at a function?

Their fashion sense is a blend of nostalgia, futuristic, and irony.

38

Why do we call Gen Z the social media detective?

They can spot a fake influencer from a mile away and aren't afraid to call them out with a perfectly placed comment!

39

How can you tell when a Gen Z person is angry?

They might start unfollowing or blocking people on social media with the speed and precision of a ninja, leaving a trail of digital casualties.

40

How can you tell when a Gen Z person is happy?

Their face lights up like a thousand Instagram filters, radiating pure joy and excitement.

41

How can you tell when
a Gen Z person has
entered the zone?

They start communicating
exclusively through GIFs
and memes, using them to
express their frustration
without uttering a
single word.

42

How can you tell when a Gen Z person can't be bothered to communicate?

They start using excessive amounts of slang and abbreviations, making it nearly impossible for anyone over the age of 25 to understand what they're saying.

43

How can you tell when a Gen Z person is creating a sense of inclusiveness?

They show off their collection of rainbow-colored clothing items that would make even a unicorn jealous.

44

When a Gen Z is feeling inclusive:

Their social media bio includes an extensive list of pronouns, including ones they've invented themselves.

45

When someone talks about the "good old days" to a Gen Z person:

They respond with an eye roll and sarcastically say, "Yeah, those were definitely the peak of humanity."

46

What did the Gen Z person say when they saw vinyl records for the first time?

This is what people used before Spotify, can you even imagine?"

47

How does Gen Z plan for the future?

They have a countdown on their phone until the day they can officially become the majority in the workforce and take over the world.

48

How do you spot a Gen Z activist?

They belong to a Gen Z-only social media platform called "GenZagram" where they can freely express their frustrations without any older generation interference.

49

What is a fashion assessor for a Gen Z person?

They carry around a vintage flip phone as a fashion accessory.

50

How many Gen Zs does it
take to change a light bulb?

None! The light bulb has
a choice to not want to
be replaced!

51

What did the Gen Zer say to
the animal control person
who was trying to catch
a squirrel?

Just climb a tree and act
like a nut!

52

Gen Zers are like walking Wi-Fi hotspots, they can't function without constant connectivity.

53

Gen Zers have a secret code language made up of emojis and acronyms. If you ever hear them say 'LOL' in a conversation, they're not actually laughing out loud, it's just a reflex.

54

Gen Zers have a sixth sense for detecting fake news. They could spot a misleading headline from a mile away, while older generations share it with all their Facebook friends.

55

Gen Zers have mastered the art of multitasking. They can watch a TikTok video, reply to a Snapchat message, and binge-watch a Netflix series all at the same time. Meanwhile, older generations struggle to find the 'on' button.

56

Gen Zers are so eco-conscious that they bring their own reusable straws to restaurants. Meanwhile, older generations are still trying to figure out how to recycle properly.

57

Gen Zers think Baby Boomers invented slow internet just to test their patience.

58

Gen Zers believe that Gen X invented the concept of 'adulting' just to make them feel overwhelmed.

59

Gen Z is convinced that Millennials invented avocado toast as a way to distract themselves from their massive student loan debt.

60

Gen Z believes that Baby Boomers' skepticism towards new technology is just their way of making sure they have an excuse to ask their grandkids for help.

61

Gen Z wonders if Millennials' obsession with self-care is just their way of avoiding the harsh reality of adult responsibilities.

62

Gen Z millionaires don't
need a yacht, they just buy
an island and call it their
'tiny home.'

63

Gen Z millionaires' idea of a 'side hustle' is starting their own space tourism company.

64

Gen Z millionaires don't buy fancy sports cars, they invest in teleportation technology instead.

65

Gen Z millionaires don't go on extravagant vacations, they just rent out entire countries for a weekend getaway.

66

Gen Z millionaires' biggest fear is not running out of money but running out of trendy slang words.

67

Gen Z millionaires' favorite pastime is playing 'Monopoly' with real properties and actual money.

68

Gen Z millionaires' version of 'retiring' is starting a charity that provides unlimited avocado toast to underprivileged Millennials.

69

Gen Z millionaires don't use regular credit cards, they pay with a custom-designed holographic payment bracelet.

70

What is the Gen Z millionaire's secret to success?

They just keep investing in meme stocks until they become the meme themselves.

71

Why did the Gen Z millionaire become a stand-up comedian?

Because they already have all the money, so they're just in it for the laughs!

72

Why did the Gen Z
millionaire start a
clothing line?

Because they needed
something to wear besides
their hoodie and joggers!

73

How does a Gen Z millionaire make decisions?

They flip a coin, but both sides have 'buy' written on them!

74

Why did the Gen Z millionaire start a food delivery service?

Because they couldn't be bothered to cook their own avocado toast!

75

How does a Gen Z millionaire celebrate their birthday?

By buying themselves a new cryptocurrency and throwing a virtual party on Zoom!

76

What's a Gen Z millionaire's go-to pickup line?

Are you a bank loan?
Because you have my
interest and I'd like to invest!'

77

How many Gen Zers does it take to change a light bulb?

None. They'd rather sit in the dark and analyze the meaning of darkness!

78

Why did the Gen Z student get an 'A' in apathy class?

Because they didn't bother to show up to class!

79

Why did the Gen Zer become a professional procrastinator?

Because they figured if they put it off long enough, they wouldn't have to care anymore!

80

Why did the Gen Zer become a professional ghoster?

To disappear from conversations.

81

Why did the Gen Zer become
a professional empath?

Because they can feel
everyone's emotions,
even the ones they
haven't met yet!"

82

How does a Gen Zer handle rejection?

They write a strongly worded letter to their own emotions, demanding an explanation!"

83

What did the Gen Z person say to their landlord for the reason they had not paid their rent in 3 months?

Be patient, once my TikTok views go viral, I will pay you.

84

What is a Gen Zer proud of?

Multitasking! A Gen Zer can procrastinate on six different platforms at once!

85

How does a Gen Zer respond when you ask them why they sleep all day?

I am not lazy! I'm just in energy-saving mode.

86

How many Gen Zers does it take to change a light bulb?

None, they prefer using LED lights.

87

Why did the Gen Zer refuse to pay for their meal?

They only use Venmo and the restaurant only accepts cash.

88

How does a Gen Zer respond to a phone call?

They let it go to voicemail and then text back immediately.

89

How many Gen Zers does it take to change a light bulb?

None, they'll just use their phones as flashlights.

90

Why did the Gen Zers bring their smartphone to the restaurant?

They wanted to take pictures of their food before eating it.

91

Why did the Gen Zer bring a ladder to the concert?

They wanted a better view for their Snapchat story.

92

Why did the Gen Zer become an astronaut?

They wanted to be the first person to take a selfie on Mars.

93

How does a Gen Zer make a decision?

They create a poll on X (formally known as Twitter) and let their followers decide.

94

How does a Gen Zer react to a phone call?

They panic and wonder why someone didn't just text them!

95

Why did the Gen Zer bring a
phone to the library?

To "check out" all the books
on Instagram.

96

How does a Gen Zer organize their closet?

By color, style, and how many likes each outfit gets on social media.

97

Why did the Gen Zer become an entrepreneur?

They wanted to create an app that solves a problem no one knew they had.

98

Why did the Gen Zer
become a chef?

They wanted to perfect
the art of making
microwaveable meals.

99

Why did the Gen Zer go to
the library?

They heard that "books"
make great props for
Instagram photos.

100

How does a Gen Zer get their news?

Through memes and viral videos, of course!

10 REASONS WE ALL NEED A BIT OF GEN Z IN US

1. **Adaptability:** Gen Z's ability to quickly adapt to change is a valuable skill in today's fast-paced world. Incorporating this trait allows us to navigate unexpected challenges and embrace new opportunities.

2. **Social awareness:** Gen Z's commitment to social causes inspires us to become more aware and engaged in issues affecting our communities. Adopting this mindset can lead to positive change and make a difference in the world.

3. **Technological literacy:** Gen Z's fluency in technology can help us stay connected, learn new skills, and leverage technology to our advantage in various aspects of life.

4. **Inclusivity:** Gen Z's inclusive mindset teaches us to value diversity and create inclusive spaces where everyone feels welcome and respected, fostering a sense of belonging and unity.

5. **Mental health prioritization:** Gen Z's emphasis on mental health serves as a reminder for us to prioritize self-care, seek support when needed, and foster a healthier relationship with our mental well-being.

6. **Entrepreneurial spirit:** Gen Z's entrepreneurial mindset encourages us to think creatively, take risks, and pursue our passions. Embracing this spirit can lead to personal and professional growth.

7. **Environmental consciousness:** Gen Z's environmental awareness inspires us to adopt sustainable practices, reduce our carbon

footprint, and contribute to a greener future for generations to come.

8. **Financial responsibility:** Gen Z's focus on financial literacy and planning encourages us to become more financially responsible, make informed decisions, and secure our financial well-being.

9. **Authenticity:** Gen Z's celebration of individuality teaches us to embrace our true selves, express our unique identities, and foster genuine connections with others.

10. **Work-life balance:** Gen Z's prioritization of work-life balance reminds us to find harmony between our personal and professional lives, leading to improved overall well-being and fulfillment.

10 THINGS WE CAN LEARN FROM GEN Z

1. **Embrace Change:** Gen Z has grown up in a fast-paced, ever-changing world. They have learned to adapt quickly, embrace new technologies, and navigate through uncertainty. They can teach us the importance of being open to change and embracing it as an opportunity for growth.

2. **Social Activism:** Gen Z is passionate about making a difference in the world. They actively engage in social and environmental causes, using their voices to advocate for change. They can teach us the power of activism and the importance of standing up for what we believe in.

3. **Technology Savviness:** Gen Z is the first true digital generation. They are tech-savvy, quick to learn new platforms, and constantly connected. They can teach us how to navigate the digital landscape, stay connected, and utilize technology to our advantage.

4. **Inclusivity and Acceptance:** Gen Z is known for its inclusive mindset and acceptance of diversity. They celebrate differences and promote equality. They can teach us the importance of embracing diversity and creating inclusive spaces where everyone feels valued.

5. **Mental Health Awareness:** Gen Z has been vocal about mental health issues, breaking the stigma surrounding them. They prioritize self-care and encourage open conversations about mental well-being. They can teach us

the importance of prioritizing mental health and seeking help when needed.

6. **Innovation:** Gen Z is driven by a desire to create their own opportunities. They are entrepreneurial and innovative, constantly finding new ways to make an impact. They can teach us the value of creativity, thinking outside the box, and pursuing our passions.

7. **Environmental Friendliness:** Gen Z is environmentally conscious and concerned about climate change. They actively promote sustainability and advocate for eco-friendly practices. They can teach us the importance of taking care of our planet and making conscious choices to reduce our environmental footprint.

8. **Budgeting:** Gen Z has grown up in a time of economic uncertainty and has learned the

value of financial responsibility. They are mindful of saving, investing, and budgeting. They can teach us the importance of financial literacy and planning for the future.

9. **Self-Expression:** Gen Z embraces individuality and self-expression. They value authenticity and are unafraid to be themselves. They can teach us the importance of embracing our true selves and expressing our unique identities.

10. **Balance:** Gen Z understands the importance of work-life balance and prioritizing well-being. They seek fulfillment in their personal lives and are not solely defined by their work. They can teach us the importance of finding balance, setting boundaries, and prioritizing our well-being.

www.ingramcontent.com/pod-product-compliance
Lightning Source LLC
Chambersburg PA
CBHW061138160726
48006CB00038B/2138